Gardening with God

---

*EVERYDAY MIRACLES IN THE
GARDENER'S LIFE*

Gene R. Stark

New Harbor Press
RAPID CITY, SD

Stark/New Harbor Press

1601 Mt Rushmore Rd, Ste 3288
Rapid City, SD 57701
www.NewHarborPress.com
Ordering Information:
Quantity sales. Special discounts are available on quantity purchases by corporations, associations, and others. For details, contact the "Special Sales Department" at the address above.

Gardening with God / Gene R. Stark —1st ed.
ISBN 978-1-63357-446-5
Gardening with God-Everyday Miracles in the Gardener's Life

Contents

Gardeners find great solace and peace in their gardens. We also find the miracles of God's grace and mercy as we study His Word and experience the wonders of His creation.

Gardens Are Special

Genesis 2:8 ⁸ And the Lord God planted a garden in Eden, in the east, and there he put the man whom he had formed.

On the sixth day of creation, God created man; His crowning finale to the creation process. Man was to oversee all of the creation, to name all the other parts of creation, to tend and take care of it all.

Where does God place Man? The answer, of course is found in Verse 8 where we are told that God planted a garden. Yes, the first Gardener was God. He felt that plants and a garden were so important that He planted a garden for Man.

I wonder if this is why we gardeners feel so comfortable in our gardens? The garden is a solace, the place of peace and relaxation. People have always planted gardens, not only for food, but for beauty and tranquility.

Just as our faith in our Savior Jesus Christ is our connection to eternity, peace, and Salvation, so our connection to the land in our gardens is our connection to a bit of earthly peace and comfort.

Prayer: Dear Lord, thank You for the gift of plants and the beauty of our gardens. Send us Your Spirit to lead us to the eternal Garden of Heaven. In Jesus' Name we pray. Amen

Spring

Text: Psalm 139:14 ¹⁴ I praise you because I am fearfully and wonderfully made; your works are wonderful, I know that full well.

T he Psalmist speaks of how fearfully and wonderfully we are made and I am led to think about how wonderfully the world is designed.

We gardeners in the northern areas look outside in March and usually we are greeted by snow, freezing temperatures, and a great deal of frost in the ground. Yet we are busy in our greenhouses starting plants which will be going outside as the weather warms. The miracle of spring is very real to us. We still have ice on our lakes, frost in the ground, and each night is still usually frosty. The design of the earth that brings the sun north each spring and quickly warms us in the lengthening days is indeed a miracle. We have faith that each year the miracle of spring will come. Just as we have faith, that with hardly a thought our hands will pick things up, so we believe in spring. Our world and our bodies are fearfully and wonderfully made.

Our faith is not just temporal. Even as our God shows us miracles each day, so the miracle of eternal life is also God's reality.

Jesus paved the way with the miracle of His Resurrection and just as the cold northern earth is resurrected each spring, so we will be resurrected.

Prayer: Dear Lord, thank you for the many miracles we experience each day. Keep us ever in the miracle of faith and Salvation. In Jesus' name we pray. Amen.

The Greatest Agreement Ever

Text: Exodus 19:4-6 [4] 'You yourselves have seen what I did to the Egyptians, and how I bore you on eagles' wings and brought you to myself. [5] Now therefore, if you will indeed obey my voice and keep my covenant, you shall be my treasured possession among all peoples, for all the earth is mine; [6] and you shall be to me a kingdom of priests and a holy nation.' These are the words that you shall speak to the people of Israel."

Text: 2 Corinthians 3:6 [6] who has made us sufficient to be ministers of a new covenant, not of the letter but of the Spirit. For the letter kills, but the Spirit gives life.

Text: Luke 22:20 [20] And likewise the cup after they had eaten, saying, "This cup that is poured out for you is the new covenant in my blood.

Each spring, as we gardeners plant our gardens, we make a silent promise to take care of our little plot. We till it, weed it, and fertilize it. We know that our garden is an expression of our devotion to the soil and to making it something to be enjoyed by others as well. We share the beauty and the produce of our garden with others as part of our promise and commitment to gardening. We hope to pass on our garden and its joy to others who come after us.

In the Old Testament God made a covenant with His people, Israel. This covenant was an agreement. God chose the people of Israel to be a special people; a people chosen to speak for God, to be ministers of His greatness and power, and to speak to the nations of the world about Him.

When Jesus the Messiah came to earth, He brought a new agreement, a new covenant with His people. This agreement is open to all mankind. Only faith, repentance, and forgiveness are required to be a member of this special group. We as Christians are chosen to be in this group. We are part of this new covenant and our special task is to proclaim the Messiah to all nations.

This wonderful agreement has been passed to us from the Old Testament and this covenant is sealed with the blood of our Savior. Each time we partake of the Holy Sacrament of Communion we renew that covenant with God and we take on anew, the responsibility of proclaiming our faith to all people.

Prayer: Dear Lord, thank you for the precious gift of faith in You and help us with Your Holy Spirit to keep the covenant by proclaiming You as Lord and God of the world. In Jesus' name we pray. Amen

The Tree of Life

Text: Ezekiel 17:22-23 [22] **Thus says the Lord GOD: "I myself will take a sprig from the lofty top of the cedar and will set it out. I will break off from the topmost of its young twigs a tender one, and I myself will plant it on a high and lofty mountain.** [23] **On the mountain height of Israel will I plant it, that it may bear branches and produce fruit and become a noble cedar. And under it will dwell every kind of bird; in the shade of its branches birds of every sort will nest.**

I f you are a gardener and have visited a garden center or nursery, you have seen a wide variety of plants. Some of these plants are grown from seeds. Many others are propagated and grown from a piece or branch cut from another larger plant. These so-called "cuttings" grow into a full-sized plant that is like the 'mother' plant. When selecting a branch from which to take a cutting, only the very best, most robust branch is selected. Any inferior or diseased branches are discarded.

The prophet Ezekiel speaks of a sprig or cutting that God has taken for the most important work of propagation in history. The sprig of a cedar tree refers to Jesus, the Messiah who was rooted into the world. Jesus, our Savior, took root into the world and His words have lived and grown for over 2000 years. The words have spread throughout the world. The words and work of redemption and salvation are meant for everyone. Jesus, the noble Cedar gives comfort, forgiveness, and salvation to everyone who seeks the shelter of his love.

Prayer: Dear Lord thank you for sending your Son, our Noble Cedar. Help us to not only seek the shelter of Jesus, but to work daily to bring others to the loving protection of His love. In Jesus' name we pray. Amen.

Soil Preparation

Text: Mark 1:1-5 [1] The beginning of the gospel of Jesus Christ, the Son of God. [2] As it is written in Isaiah the prophet, "Behold, I send my messenger before your face, who will prepare your way, [3] the voice of one crying in the wilderness: 'Prepare the way of the Lord,
make his paths straight,'" [4] John appeared, baptizing in the wilderness and proclaiming a baptism of repentance for the forgiveness of sins. [5] And all the country of Judea and all Jerusalem were going out to him and were being baptized by him in the river Jordan, confessing their sins.

Gardeners know the importance of preparation. When gardening season arrives, it is best to have everything ready. All the seeds, tools, fertilizers, and other gardening materials need to be at hand. When the time and weather are right, it is important to get into the garden to begin the new season. It is especially important to prepare the soil for planting. The soil needs to be worked and brought to a consistency which is good for planting. Cultivation and tilling prepare the way for planting the seeds and young plants.

John the Baptist was sent by God to prepare the way for Jesus. John's message of repentance, forgiveness, and baptism laid the ground work for the message proclaimed by Jesus. John the

Baptist prepared the people for the Messiah and His work of salvation for all mankind. Jesus' future disciples were aware of John and his special message of repentance and forgiveness. The importance of preparation cannot be underestimated. Likewise, Jesus prepared His followers to carry the message of salvation to the "ends of the earth." Now the Word and Holy Spirit prepare the hearts of all believers to continue the work of evangelism.

Prayer: Dear Lord, prepare us each day to carry out the work of proclaiming the salvation won by Jesus' life, death, and resurrection. Send us your Spirit and open your word to our understanding. In Jesus' name we pray. Amen

Pruning Grapes

Reading: John 15: 1-8 [1] "I am the true vine, and my Father is the vinedresser. [2] Every branch in me that does not bear fruit he takes away, and every branch that does bear fruit he prunes, that it may bear more fruit. [3] Already you are clean because of the word that I have spoken to you. [4] Abide in me, and I in you. As the branch cannot bear fruit by itself, unless it abides in the vine, neither can you, unless you abide in me. [5] I am the vine; you are the branches. Whoever abides in me and I in him, he it is that bears much fruit, for apart from me you can do nothing. [6] If anyone does not abide in me he is thrown away like a branch and withers; and the branches are gathered, thrown into the fire, and burned. [7] If you abide in me, and my words abide in you, ask whatever you wish, and it will be done for you. [8] By this my Father is glorified, that you bear much fruit and so prove to be my disciples.

I have planted grapes in my garden. After building a trellising system, I trained the vines up and then horizontally along the wires. Each vine needed to be trained and pruned. I learned that some vines grow rapidly, stretching out with few buds between long stretches of smooth vine. These are often called "bull canes" and they have little potential to produce good quantities of fruit. They grow rapidly and quickly stretch out far from the true vine and they lack the fruit-bearing nourishment of the central vine. They need to be pruned from the vine.

I have learned to prune the new growth close to the central vine. Upon these branches the buds are close together and many clusters of fruit will be produced by these branches.

Often the words of Jesus are very much in touch with gardeners and horticulturalists. He understands gardening and the process of growing grapes. He described how the central vine of a grape plant nourishes the fruit-producing vines. We Christians, as His followers, must stay close to Him. He is the True Vine and if we, the branches, are to bear spiritual fruit, we must remain close to Him. We must be continuously nourished by the Word of Life. Only when we are constantly nourished by the Word can we bear the fruit of witnessing to others about Salvation in Christ.

Prayer: Dear Lord help us to be branches who grow close to the True Vine. Nourish us with Your Word and strengthen our faith. In Jesus' Name we pray. Amen.

Rooting Cuttings

Text: Isaiah 11:1-2 [1] There shall come forth a shoot from the stump of Jesse, and a branch from his roots shall bear fruit. [2] And the Spirit of the LORD shall rest upon him, the Spirit of wisdom and understanding, the Spirit of counsel and might, the Spirit of knowledge and the fear of the LORD.

Gardeners know about rooting cuttings. Some plants need to be propagated by rooting cuttings. Taking a piece of a plant and getting that piece to form roots by putting the piece into either soil or water, is how we often start new plants. I know that I can take a piece of a favorite grape vine and stick it into potting soil to produce a new grape plant. The new plant will be a perfect duplication of the parent plant, yet it will be a different plant. Sometimes we can simply break a shoot from a growing root and plant this shoot in a new place and it will grow to be a new, thriving plant.

In the reading from Isaiah it was foretold that a shoot will come from the stump of Jesse, a descendant of David. This new shoot is the promised Messiah and it will bear fruit, just as a new cutting will take root and grow into a productive plant. The Messiah, namely Jesus, will have the Spirit of the land resting upon Him and He will be filled with wisdom and understanding, counsel and light, the Spirit of knowledge and the fear of the Lord. Just as the fresh new vigor of a young plant causes it to grow rapidly and produce abundant fruit, so the Messiah will be a new and abundant blessing to all the world.

As we see the promises and prophecy of Isaiah unfold into the new life and abundant grace of our Savior, we realize the fulfillment of God's promise of Salvation.

Prayer: Dear Lord, we thank You for the lineage of David through which You paved the way for our Savior Jesus to come into the world. Send us Your Spirit to keep us in the true faith. In Jesus' name we pray. Amen

The Essence of Life

Text: 1Peter 1:22-25 [22] Having purified your souls by your obedience to the truth for a sincere brotherly love, love one another earnestly from a pure heart, [23] since you have been born again, not of perishable seed but of imperishable, through the living and abiding word of God; [24] for "All flesh is like grass and all its glory like the flower of grass. The grass withers, and the flower falls, [25] but the word of the Lord remains forever." And this word is the good news that was preached to you.

Have you ever considered the wonderful miracle of seed? It is produced when the plant dies and the flower wilts. Yet the seed is hard and immovable. Within that seed is an imperishable germ of Life.

I know from experience, as a gardener who has germinated many seeds that they contain a stubborn, indeed imperishable essence of life. Some native plants can lie dormant in the soil for years and still eventually germinate and produce a new living plant.

We as believing and forgiving Christians are like seed. We have been produced by the loving work of redemption of Jesus

Christ and are now ready to be re-born, that is geminated into the eternal and imperishable eternity provided by God.

Prayer: Dear Lord, make us thankful each day, as we experience the miracle of our gardens. Teach us through our gardens that You have saved us to be imperishable seed as forgiven and re-deemed saints. In Jesus name we pray. Amen

Looking for a Sign

Text: Isaiah 7:14 [14] Therefore the Lord himself will give you a sign. Behold, the virgin shall conceive and bear a son, and shall call his name Immanuel.

Text: Mathew 12:38-40 [38] Then some of the scribes and Pharisees answered him, saying, "Teacher, we wish to see a sign from you." [39] But he answered them, "An evil and adulterous generation seeks for a sign, but no sign will be given to it except the sign of the prophet Jonah. [40] For just as Jonah was three days and three nights in the belly of the great fish, so will the Son of Man be three days and three nights in the heart of the earth.

Avid gardeners often get asked about when is the right time to plant tomato plants outside. I used to respond with tongue in cheek, "plant them the day after the last frost." Of course, here in the North Country it's impossible to know for sure when the last frost has occurred. Maybe a better sign of when to plant tomatoes is what I was told by an old gardener, "Plant them when the oak leaves are the size of mouse ears." It is comforting to have a 'sign.' Something we can go by.

Isaiah gives us a sign about the coming Messiah, who will be born of a virgin and will be named Immanuel. Jesus, the Messiah was also asked for a sign to prove that He was the Messiah. Jesus refers to the Old Testament prophet Jonah, who was in the belly of the fish for three days and nights. It is the sign of Jesus who was crucified, buried for three days, and rose again on the third day. This is our sign of salvation for on the third day Jesus proclaimed victory over sin and death for all believers. This is the greatest sign we could ask for.

Prayer: Dear Lord, thank You for all the great signs and wonders proclaimed to us in Your Word in the Old and New Testaments. Send us Your Spirit to enrich our understanding of these signs. In Jesus' name we pray. Amen

Promises, Promises

Text: Isaiah 55:10-11 [10] **"For as the rain and the snow come down from heaven, and do not return there but water the earth, making it bring forth and sprout, giving seed to the sower and bread to the eater,** [11] **so shall my word be that goes out from my mouth; it shall not return to me empty, but it shall accomplish that which I purpose, and shall succeed in the thing for which I sent it.**

Gardeners are dependent upon promises. The promises are as old as time and as plain and understandable as black and white. We depend upon the promise of spring. We know that as the days lengthen, the temperatures get warmer and with the temperatures, the soil warms. The promise of seed in warm soil is that germination will take place. We depend upon the promise of the sun, with its bright warmth that plants will photosynthesize and grow green and lush. We also depend upon the promise of rain and snow to water the land.

We have also a promise from God that His Word will produce results. The power of God's Word is as sure as the promise that sun and rain will cause our gardens to grow. When God's Word is preached and shared it will get results. The Word of Life is indeed the promise of Life eternal and that Word will instill faith into the hearts of mankind. The saving grace of our Savior is clearly spelled out in the Word. The Word will accomplish its purpose.

Prayer: Dear Lord, we thank You for Your holy Word and its promise of results. Help us to share the Word and its promise of Life eternal. In Jesus' Name we pray. Amen.

Straight Rows

Text: Luke 9:61-62 [61] Yet another said, "I will follow you, Lord, but let me first say farewell to those at my home." [62] Jesus said to him, "No one who puts his hand to the plow and looks back is fit for the kingdom of God."

Gardeners and farmers operate various types of equipment to till and cultivate the soil. Tillage equipment requires that the operator be fully attentive to the job at hand. There is no time to be looking back or around and not paying attention to what one is doing. One must always look forward to steer in a straight line. If you travel with farmers out in farm country, they will always be observing and commenting on the straightness of the field rows. Farmers take pride in straight and organized fields. Gardeners also use various techniques to keep rows straight.

Jesus knew the importance of always looking ahead and paying attention to what is in front of us. He called disciples to follow Him and laid out the importance of looking forward, keeping their eye on the row; focusing upon the future and not the past. As Christians we are called to do the same, for the future is exciting. The future of love and joy in eternal life through the redemption bought with Jesus' blood is indeed worth focusing upon. We must always look to the cross and the precious Salvation ahead which is ours through Christ.

Prayer: Dear Lord, help us to always keep our eye on the important mission with which we are entrusted. Help us to focus upon Your Word and the gift of Salvation which is ours. In Jesus' name we pray. Amen

Seeds of Glory

Text: 1 Corinthians 15:35-38 [35] But someone will ask, "How are the dead raised? With what kind of body do they come?" [36] You foolish person! What you sow does not come to life unless it dies. [37] And what you sow is not the body that is to be, but a bare kernel, perhaps of wheat or of some other grain. [38] But God gives it a body as he has chosen, and to each kind of seed its own body.

We Gardeners know about seeds. In our gardens we all plant many and various kinds of seeds. It is obvious to us that the seed we plant into the soil, has no resemblance to the plant that is produced.

A round, hard, and very tiny petunia seed looks nothing like the bright flowering plant we will have from it later in the season. The seeds we plant absorb moisture and their exterior skin wrinkles and rots as the inside of the seed expands and begins to grow. The seed actually dies as it transitions to a new and much more impressive life. The tiny seed grows into a large green plant which flowers in miraculous colors.

Paul says in First Corinthians that we Christians also will go through this transition. The body we have is only a seed; a tiny beginning of the wondrous body God will have for us in eternity. It will be a glorious transition. What joy and thankfulness we will experience in this transition, made possible by the death and resurrection of our Savior, Jesus.

Pray: Dear lord, Thank You for making a path for all believers to transition into the eternal glory of Heaven. Keep us in faith and focus us upon the beauty You will work in us for all eternity. In Jesus' name we pray. Amen

Watching the Weather

Text: Mathew 16:1-4 [1] And the Pharisees and Sadducees came, and to test him they asked him to show them a sign from heaven. [2] He answered them, "When it is evening, you say, 'It will be fair weather, for the sky is red.' [3] And in the morning, 'It will be stormy today, for the sky is red and threatening.' You know how to interpret the appearance of the sky, but you cannot interpret the signs of the times. [4] An evil and adulterous generation seeks for a sign, but no sign will be given to it except the sign of Jonah." So, he left them and departed.

Gardeners tend to keep a close eye on the weather. They look for rain clouds to bring water to a thirsty garden. Gardeners also keep an eye out for treacherous storms that could bring hail and heavy downpours which might damage their gardens. Gardeners become good at interpreting the signs of the weather and predicting what kind of conditions to expect. By observing the clouds and the sky, they can predict what is coming.

The church leaders of Jesus' time demanded that He give them a sign that He was the Savior. He said that the signs were already before them, just as the signs of weather were evident each day. All they had to do was observe the miracles and the wondrous words He spoke. The greatest sign was the sign of Jonah; the sign of death as Jonah was swallowed by the fish and then thrown back up alive, pointing to Jesus' death and resurrection. We have Scriptural proof of the miraculous work of salvation. As Paul writes in 1 Corinthians, "The Jews demand signs… but we preach Christ Crucified." The sign of the Resurrection is our sign of eternal life and salvation.

Prayer: Dear Lord, we thank You for the greatest sign in history, the resurrection of Jesus and by it the assurance of our resurrection as well. In Jesus' name we pray. Amen

The Solace of the Garden

Text: John 18:1-3 [1] **When Jesus had spoken these words, he went out with his disciples across the brook Kidron, where there was a garden, which he and his disciples entered.** [2] **Now Judas, who betrayed him, also knew the place, for Jesus often met there with his disciples.** [3] **So Judas, having procured a band of soldiers and some officers from the chief priests and the Pharisees, went there with lanterns and torches and weapons.**

How often do we gardeners complete a day's work at our regular occupation, change into our gardening clothes, and go to our garden? We are attracted to our quiet solace where plants grow. It is the place where we tend our vegetables and fruits, where we admire our flowers, and find peace and contentment at the end of a long day. I like to think of evenings as one of the most wonderful times to be in the garden. Even when I spent long days in my vegetables when I was growing produce for market, I still enjoyed my evening walks in the garden. It was a time to see the plants drink in the evening air and breathe their soothing aroma as I enjoyed the quiet time when workers had gone for the day and tractors and other equipment were silent.

The garden is more than a source of food, it a source of peace. Our Savior Jesus also knew the peace and quietude that a garden can provide. Our text tells us that Jesus often went to the garden with His disciples. The Garden of Gethsemane was a place where they met, perhaps a place where they even camped among the olive trees.

As Jesus began His journey to the cross, He went to the garden to pray. In this setting of evening quietude, He earnestly prayed to the Father for strength to complete the greatest task ever embarked upon. The peace and strength of prayer in the garden points us to the eternal peace and strength of our resurrected Savior.

Prayer: Dear Lord, thank You for gardens. Thank You for a Savior who went to the garden and then to the cross to complete the work of Salvation. In Jesus' name we pray. Amen

The Biggest Tomatoes

Text: 1Corinthians 15:17-23 [17] And if Christ has not been raised, your faith is futile and you are still in your sins. [18] Then those also who have fallen asleep in Christ have perished. [19] If in Christ we have hope in this life only, we are of all people most to be pitied. [20] But in fact Christ has been raised from the dead, the firstfruits of those who have fallen asleep. [21] For as by a man came death, by a man has come also the resurrection of the dead. [22] For as in Adam all die, so also in Christ shall all be made alive. [23] But each in his own order: Christ the firstfruits, then at his coming those who belong to Christ.

Gardeners all await with great anticipation, the first ripe tomatoes of the season. These first tomatoes tend to be the largest, and best of the whole year. As we take them from the vine we anticipate the flavor and juiciness of these "first fruits."

Paul refers to Jesus as the "first fruits" of all who have fallen asleep. In other words, He is the first to have the power over death. Jesus alone has the power to be raised from the dead and to raise all believers from death.

Our text points out that the very essence of our faith is in the resurrection. Our faith would be futile and of little value if it was only a temporal faith. But through Jesus our faith is eternal. The sin of Adam brought death into the world and death for all, yet in Christ all shall be made alive! He is indeed the "first fruits," the One who brings eternal life to all who believe in His promise.

Prayer: Dear Lord thank You for allowing all Christians to share in the delicious "first fruits" of eternal life. In Jesus' name we pray. Amen.

Rooted and Established

Text: Ephesians 3:17-19 [17] **so that Christ may dwell in your hearts through faith—that you, being rooted and grounded in love,** [18] **may have strength to comprehend with all the saints what is the breadth and length and height and depth,** [19] **and to know the love of Christ that surpasses knowledge, that you may be filled with all the fullness of God.**

Soil is a complex and wonderful thing. It really goes beyond our knowledge. Yet plants are able to grow and thrive in the soil in our gardens. We know that when we place plants or seeds into soil these plants will grow and bear fruit. Once the plants are rooted, once those roots reach out into the soil, the crop is well on its way to success.

Once Christians are rooted in the love of Christ, miracles begin to happen. The miraculous 'soil' of the love of Christ is what roots the Christian life. Just as the mystery of plants rooted in good soil brings forth fruit, so also our lives as Christians grow and prosper. We cannot fully comprehend the miraculous attributes of soil, nor can we fully grasp the full implication of God's love. The reality is that Jesus was willing to suffer and die on a cross to insure forgiveness and salvation for all of us sinners.

Indeed, such love surpasses knowledge. Just as we don't need to fully understand how soil can grow our plants, we don't need to fully understand the love of God; only believe and accept His forgiveness.

Prayer: Dear Lord, there are so many mysteries in the world. Thank You for a love that surpassed all understanding. Send us Your Spirit and keep us in the faith. In Jesus' Name we pray. Amen

Weeds!

Text: Mathew 13:24-30 [24] He put another parable before them, saying, "The kingdom of heaven may be compared to a man who sowed good seed in his field, [25] but while his men were sleeping, his enemy came and sowed weeds among the wheat and went away. [26] So when the plants came up and bore grain, then the weeds appeared also. [27] And the servants of the master of the house came and said to him, 'Master, did you not sow good seed in your field? How then does it have weeds?' [28] He said to them, 'An enemy has done this.' So the servants said to him, 'Then do you want us to go and gather them?' [29] But he said, 'No, lest in gathering the weeds you root up the wheat along with them. [30] Let both grow together until the harvest, and at harvest time I will tell the reapers, "Gather the weeds first and bind them in bundles to be burned, but gather the wheat into my barn."'"

Weeds are a great bane to all gardeners. We hoe them, we till them out, we pull them, and some even spray them with herbicides. Yet they always seem to survive, they are always with us. We sometimes wonder where they all come from. As in the text, they are found among our desirable plants. Weeds seem to purposefully entwine their roots around the roots of our vegetables and flowers. There are times when we cannot pull the weeds out without fear of uprooting our garden plants. Only at harvest time can these weeds be pulled and destroyed.

God's garden was created in perfection, but through the work of the Devil, sin infested the world. In God's garden, those who have accepted God's saving grace from sin, live in the constant blessing of God's forgiveness. Yet the Forgiven live among those who have rejected God's forgiveness. In many ways our lives are entwined with the lives of those who have not accepted Christ. Unbelievers are found at work, in government, and everywhere we go. Yet God pours down His daily grace upon all people. The constant hope that all will accept Christ is always alive. Yet the harvest will come. It is God's judgement upon all people. At that point all believers will be separated from the unbelievers. God's harvest will come, and His perfect garden in heaven will be the home of all believers.

Prayer: Dear Lord thank You for the constant opportunity to witness to all people around us. Help us to let our light shine and share the Word of Life with the world. In Jesus' name we pray. Amen.

The Waiting is the Hardest Part

Text: James 5:7-8 **⁷ Be patient, therefore, brothers, until the coming of the Lord. See how the farmer waits for the precious fruit of the earth, being patient about it, until it receives the early and the late rains. ⁸ You also, be patient. Establish your hearts, for the coming of the Lord is at hand.**

I remember a gardening year when I planted a large patch of tomatoes. I weeded and mulched and side-dressed with compost. The tomatoes grew nicely and bloomed. During the early part of the summer the moisture in the soil was adequate, yet as the summer wore on, no rain fell.

Having learned that tomatoes take some time to set fruit and mature, I waited for the crop to materialize. The heat of summer began to take its toll on my tomatoes. I waited and each day looked to the sky for sign of a shower of rain.

Finally, as the tomato leaves curled in the heat and drought, I saw clouds to the west and miraculously a shower came up and dropped a wonderful rainfall. The results were almost instantaneous. The tomato leaves no longer were curled and parched. The green color of the plants became deep and healthy as fruit set upon the vines. The one generous rainfall saved the parched vines and produced an abundant crop.

We as Christians wait on the Lord. Some days we feel parched by war, terrorism, and lawlessness. We wonder how long before the Lord returns to set it all right. Yet, just as the rain came to save my garden so too the Lord will return to save His Redeemed people.

Prayer: Lord we pray: "Come Lord Jesus," yet not our will but Yours be done. Only You know the right time and place. Give us patience and faith to submit to your will. In Jesus' name we pray. Amen

19

August Abundance

Text: Luke 10:2 ² And he said to them, "The harvest is plentiful, but the laborers are few. Therefore pray earnestly to the Lord of the harvest to send out laborers into his harvest.

A s I write this, it's August. The word "august" means 'important.' August is indeed appropriately named, and it is especially important if we are gardeners. It is truly the biggest month of harvest for vegetable gardeners. All the wonderful and delicious delights of fresh vegetables and fruit seem to be in season during August.

The harvest is great and therefore extra time and work are required to get the produce picked and prepared. Canning, freezing, and other means of preserving the harvest must be done. Certainly, the month of August came to mind as I read our text. The harvest is great!

Our Lord often referenced gardening and farming as He spoke to His followers. They knew the implications of a large harvest. They knew from experience and observation that a great harvest required many workers to the get the job done.

The harvest of souls is also great as we look into the world. There is so much to be done, so many souls in need of the Gospel message. We must do our part and our prayer must be that God, the Lord of the harvest, send enough workers to get the job done.

Prayer: Dear Lord, your work of salvation is the most important work on earth. Each soul is precious and needs the Gospel. Give us a full measure of wisdom and stamina as we work in Your harvest, and send ample laborers into the harvest. In Jesus' Name we pray. Amen.

20

A Million Dollar Rain

Text: Isaiah 45:8 "Shower, O heavens, from above, and let the clouds rain down righteousness; let the earth open, that salvation and righteousness may bear fruit; let the earth cause them both to sprout; I the LORD have created it.

Growing up as a child, I remember summers when the sun seemed to shine almost every day. Few clouds appeared and to a child growing up it seemed wonderful to have every day to go outside to swim and fish and never get rained upon. Yet to farmers and gardeners the continuous days of clear weather were troubling. We depended upon rain to water the crops.

I also remember when the clouds built up in the west and the weather seemed extremely humid. Soon the lightning and thunder would arrive and rain would fall. When the rain came steady and soaked into the earth, I can still remember my Dad saying, "It's a million-dollar rain." A million dollars seemed like an incredible amount of money to me as a child. It was in fact an incomprehensible amount of money and it seemed like the rain must have been miraculous to bring such results. Usually in church the next Sunday, the pastor would give thanks to God for the rainfall.

Isaiah refers to clouds raining down righteousness. He refers to the fruits of a shower as righteousness and salvation. All credit is given to God for this salvation, and the forgiveness we enjoy.

God has rained upon all believers as he sent his only Son upon the earth to bring the fruits of salvation for all, with His atonement on the cross of Calvary. What a priceless gift God has rained upon all humanity; an endless supply of righteousness and forgiveness to all who believe.

Prayer: Dear Lord we thank You for Your gracious shower of forgiveness and Salvation. Keep us ever mindful of Your endless grace. In Jesus' name we pray. Amen.

Smothering Weeds

Texts:

Psalm 32:1 Blessed is the one whose transgression is forgiven, whose sin is covered.

Romans 4:7-8 [7] "Blessed are those whose lawless deeds are forgiven,
and whose sins are covered; [8] blessed is the man against whom the Lord will not count his sin."

1 Peter 4:8 [8] Above all, keep loving one another earnestly, since love covers a multitude of sins.

I was working in my garden, specifically in my potato patch. I worked with my hoe, drawing soil up around the base of each plant. The soil I moved, covered many weeds that were beginning to grow. The soil effectively covered the weeds, smothering them out and allowing my potatoes to grow and prosper without the weed competition.

The soil flowing around my plants reminded me of the love of Christ which flows over us and effectively covers all our sins. His precious blood, shed in love on the cross of Calvary is the remedy for all of our sins and this powerful covering allows us to prosper without the guilt of sin. We are kept clean and forgiven as we daily repent and welcome the love of Jesus into our lives.

Prayer: Dear Lord, we thank You for the covering of forgiveness. Teach us each day to live in the joy of repentance and forgiveness. In Jesus' name we pray. Amen.

The Patient Gardener

Text: Luke 13: 6-9 [6] And he told this parable: "A man had a fig tree planted in his vineyard, and he came seeking fruit on it and found none. [7] And he said to the vinedresser, 'Look, for three years now I have come seeking fruit on this fig tree, and I find none. Cut it down. Why should it use up the ground?'[8] And he answered him, 'Sir, let it alone this year also, until I dig around it and put on manure. [9] Then if it should bear fruit next year, well and good; but if not, you can cut it down.'"

Fruit production is very important to gardeners. We plant fruit trees, vegetables, and other fruiting plants because we expect to get a yield of sweet juicy fruit.

We now live in Minnesota but when we lived a bit further south in Nebraska we felt there was the possibility of growing sweet, juicy peaches. Peaches are indeed a wonderful fruit when picked ripened and fresh from the tree. We struggled with the peaches. Even though we planted varieties that are deemed hardy for the zone, an abnormally cold winter would destroy the fruiting buds. Another season would see the buds survive and a beautiful bloom would happen, only to be nipped by a spring frost. It would have been easy to give up and put a reliable apple tree in the peach tree's place. Yet, we persevered and did eventually harvest some truly sweet and juicy fruit.

The fruit of faith and forgiveness is indeed the greatest harvest to be had. It is an eternal harvest that ensures the salvation of souls. As a Christian bears witness of his faith to others, there is always the discouragement of those who will not open their hearts to the message of the Word. There are those who are too busy to be bothered with church and Bible study. Yet we are reminded by Christ in the text that we need to persevere. We must be like the patient gardener in the text who fertilized and weeded and pruned the tree. The rewards are eternal and worth the extra effort.

Prayer: Dear Lord, give us the patience to preserver as witnesses to the Word of Life. Bless our efforts and send Your Spirit to those who hear the Word. In Jesus' name we pray. Amen.

God's Gentle Rain on All

Text: Matt. 5: 43-45 [43] "You have heard that it was said, 'You shall love your neighbor and hate your enemy.' [44] But I say to you, Love your enemies and pray for those who persecute you, [45] so that you may be sons of your Father who is in heaven. For he makes his sun rise on the evil and on the good, and sends rain on the just and on the unjust.

Weather is so important to gardeners. Each and every one of us listens to the weather forecast. We know that the weather determines the success of our gardens. The right temperatures and of course the correct amount of rain can determine whether we have mediocre yields or abundant crops.

No matter how hard we work at weeding, fertilizing, and caring for our gardens, in the end the weather still plays an important role in our gardening success. When the weather is just right, everybody has a good garden, even those who perhaps have weeds in their patch or who may have neglected to properly trellis their tomatoes. When all of us share in a good gardening season, even those who may not have spent as much time and effort caring for their garden, we should all rejoice and be glad for the abundant harvest.

Jesus pointed out the fact that we are all sinners, we all have the common fault of original sin. None of us is perfect. We all need a Savior. Just as the thief on the cross was saved by a simple act of faith on the day of his death, so we are all saved by the same faith. God's mercy is there for all, just as His precious rain and sunshine blesses the gardens of all people.

Prayer: Dear Lord, Thank You for the great love and grace that enfolds all people. Lead us to the saving faith that saves all sinners. In Jesus' Name we pray. Amen.

Not Just the Valleys

Text: Psalm 147:7-8 ⁷ **Sing to the LORD with thanksgiving; make melody to our God on the lyre!** ⁸ **He covers the heavens with clouds; he prepares rain for the earth; he makes grass grow on the hills.**

Some of us have gardened in the valleys. We have experienced the deep, dark soil; the alluvial wealth that only cropland in the rich, well-watered valleys can bring. Growing crops in the hill country is not the sure thing that those in the well-watered valleys experience. Drought can stunt and turn to brown the cropland and grassland of the hills. Those who depend upon the hill-lands for their livelihood, look often to the horizon for the clouds that give promise of rain. During the growing season these folks often, utter words of prayer for the refreshing rain to keep the hills green.

Certainly, we must all give thanks to God for seasonal weather and His blessing upon the crops. Yet we have a God who is not only capable of the easy blessings. We have a God who brings rain to the hills, a God who can green-up the highlands.

Indeed, we have a God who took on the most difficult of all tasks. He made a way for the sin-stained world to be cleansed to perfection. He sent a Savior, His only son, to take upon Himself all the evil of the world and destroy it by His loving act of salvation on the cross of Calvary.

We sing to the Lord with thanksgiving, for He can make the driest hills green and save for eternity even the most wretched sinner.

Prayer: Lord thank You for being such an awesome God. Keep us in the faith by Your Spirit. In Jesus' name we pray. Amen

Rooted in the Word of Life

Text: Jeremiah 17:7-8 "Blessed is the man who trusts in the LORD, whose trust is the LORD.

8 He is like a tree planted by water, that sends out its roots by the stream, and does not fear when heat comes, for its leaves remain green, and is not anxious in the year of drought, for it does not cease to bear fruit."

I once talked with a vegetable grower who farmed in an area of Florida where the land was sub-irrigated. In other words, the water table was high enough that the roots of his crop could always reach down into the soil and find water. No matter how little rain fell on the land, his crop never failed because there was always water below the soil for his crops to tap.

Our faith is also blessed like the farmer's sub-irrigated fields. If we put our trust in the Lord, and know that His Holy Word is always there to sustain us and to water our faith we will always bear spiritual fruit. Like a tree planted near a steam, we will always have a source of life. Even as we are ravaged by perils, His Word will always be there for us.

Prayer: Dear Lord, Thank You for Your sustaining Word. Help us to always tap into it to sustain us in our faith. In Jesus' Name we pray. Amen.

26

Dead-heading our Lives

Text: 1Peter 1:24-25 ²⁴ for "All flesh is like grass and all its glory like the flower of grass. The grass withers, and the flower falls, ²⁵ but the word of the Lord remains forever." And this word is the good news that was preached to you.

Gardeners know what dead-heading is all about, especially those of us who love flowers and grow colorful beds of annuals. We know that to keep the flower beds looking bright and beautiful, we need to dead-head the flowers; we need to pick the spent and brown blooms off the plants. Even the most gorgeous of roses, the most spectacular petunias, and the most dazzling geranium blooms eventually wilt and turn to a drab shade of brown or black.

People are no different. No matter how famous we may become, no matter what prestigious positions we ascend to, we know what awaits all of mankind in the end.

Miraculously, we have the power to overcome the inevitable. The dead-heading of temporal death confronts all, yet we have the Word of the Lord which remains the same forever. It is the saving Word that has been preached to us: The Good News that we can overcome the inevitable and attain eternal brightness and life through the saving mercy of Jesus.

Prayer: Dear Lord, thank you for giving us your powerful Word that leads us to eternal Life. In Jesus' name we pray. Amen.

27

The First Fruits

Text: 1Corinthians 15:20 But in fact Christ has been raised from the dead, the firstfruits of those who have fallen asleep.

Only gardeners know the joy of the first delicious, vine-ripened tomatoes. They also know about the muskmelon that sets on the vine ahead of the other fruits, and how they watch it grow, and how its skin roughens and finally it begins to turn from green to a creamy-yellow color. Soon a hint of the sweet smell of melon fills the air and finally with a slight tug the stem separates from the melon. The pleasant memory of the first slice and its sweet, musky flavor lingers. The first zucchini sautéed with onion, the first cucumber so fresh and juicy, or the new potato robbed from under the plant, are all remarkable first fruits in our gardening experience. There is nothing better than the first fruits because they fulfill all the wonderful anticipation that we gardeners enjoy.

In first Corinthians Paul speaks of Jesus as the 'firstfruits.' Paul was raised in the Jewish traditions and knew that throughout the Old Testament Scripture, the promise of a coming Messiah was a focal point. Paul had come to realize that Jesus is that promised Messiah. The resurrection of Jesus was the first fruits of all believers. Just as He came from the grave on Easter, so now all believers will also follow. Jesus' resurrection will be participated in by all believers. Just as tomatoes continue to ripen on the vines and melons continue to be produced during the summer, so we too will follow Christ to Eternal Salvation.

Prayer: Dear Lord, as we experience the seasonal first fruits in our gardens, so too we are thankful for our Savior, the eternal 'firstfruits.' Ever strengthen our faith and anticipation of your eternal love and gift of salvation. In Jesus' name we pray. Amen.

28

Keeping Up with the Work

Text: 1Thessalonians 5:16-18 16 Rejoice always, [17] pray without ceasing, [18] give thanks in all circumstances; for this is the will of God in Christ Jesus for you.

Gardeners know how important it is to keep up with the work. Weeds need to be constantly pulled. Soil needs to be cultivated and new plantings need to be established on a regular schedule. Continually keeping up with the work assures us of prolonged beauty in our flower beds and also a bountiful harvest. Some days we may not feel like hoeing and pulling weeds, but we need to keep up.

Paul's words to the Thessalonians stressed the constant and joyful need to keep up our spiritual life. Praying and rejoicing, some days is not that easy to do. Stress, cares, and concerns invade our lives. Yet the love of God which was shown to us in the redeeming work of Christ is always a reason to rejoice. What about praying without ceasing? Like gardening, it seems like a full-time job, nearly impossible to complete. Yet our daily breath is a prayer each time we inhale. Each step we take each day is a prayer of thanks as we make our way through life. Each challenge at work, in school, or in our home life is a prayer for God's guidance and support. Our hearts connect to our God and Savior each minute of each day as His breath of life feeds our body and soul. We need to keep Him close, a constant partner in our daily walk.

Paul knew the challenges of life, of sin and forgiveness, and joy in the love of God. He knew the value of ceaseless prayer and constant reliance upon our gracious and forgiving God.

Prayer: Dear Lord, keep us always close as we come to you in ceaseless prayer. Send us Your Spirit minute by minute and day by day to strengthen our faith. In Jesus' name we pray. Amen

29

Wildflowers

Text: Mathew 6:28-29: [28] And why are you anxious about clothing? Consider the lilies of the field, how they grow: they neither toil nor spin, [29] yet I tell you, even Solomon in all his glory was not arrayed like one of these.

I t is late summer and as I gaze from my formal planting in my yard and look to the wild, native prairie which stretches behind our house, I realize that my hard work in the formal garden has been outdone by the random native flowers growing unattended in the wild prairie. No one has hoed or cultivated these wildflowers, yet coneflowers, black-eyed Susans, and beebalm dance in the summer breeze and punctuate the native stands of big bluestem grass.

Jesus often points out examples in the outdoors that teach us a lesson. He knew the beauty of the wildflowers and He also knew that no one cultivated these stunningly beautiful flowers. Yet they thrive and radiate color and brightness that even kings would envy. He is not saying we gardeners should quit hoeing and cultivating our gardens. Yet He reassures us with His words that we need not worry or fret. We are promised that God is always with us. Yet the great lesson here is not one of temporal satisfaction of our bodily needs but more important that God is with us. The Salvation given to us by Christ's death and resurrection is a sure thing. We need only accept it. Forgiveness and salvation are as free a gift as the beautiful colors of the wildflowers. We are His people and His creation. He has a certain plan for our spiritual well-being.

Payer: Dear Lord, Thank you for your ever-present love and protection. Even as the wild flowers bloom, keep our faith ever alive, with the beautiful colors of love, repentance, and forgiveness. In Jesus' name we pray. Amen

30

A God for all our Needs

Text: Psalm 104:14-15 [14] **You cause the grass to grow for the livestock and plants for man to cultivate, that he may bring forth food from the earth** [15] **and wine to gladden the heart of man, oil to make his face shine and bread to strengthen man's heart.**

I'll have to admit that I am an avid gardener. In fact, I am a crazily diverse gardener. I get my fingers dirty in a lot of places. I grow vegetables because I like to eat them. It doesn't stop there. I must have some flowers because summer is so short and I need the vibrant colors of flowers to brighten the season. Of course, herbs are necessary when I cook. I have native plants because they are beautiful and I want to help our bee and butterfly pollinators. Berries and melons; of course! Now I have also expanded into grapes and each September ushers in a bit of crushing and fermentation. I make some wine to gladden the heart of man!

My gardening has expanded from the first asparagus that snaps off so crisp and flavorful in spring to early cole crops and lettuces, and going on through new potatoes, tomatoes and peppers, finally rounding out with winter squash and the persistent kale that hangs on until November most years. The greenhouse takes my gardening to a new level and expands my growing to four seasons.

Our God is a "four seasons" God. His goodness gives us forage for livestock, food for us, and all manner of blessings to keep us. Yet His mercy is not only for the seasons of the earth but His mercy goes beyond the bounds of earthly time. Through the redeeming work of Jesus, the blessings of life extend to eternity. The greatest blessings are still ahead. God's love for us is eternal.

Prayer: Dear Lord, thank You for all blessings both temporal and eternal. Send us Your Spirit to constantly point us to the abundant and eternal garden earned for us on the cross of Calvary. In Jesus' name we pray. Amen.

Thumping Melons

Text: John 4:35-38 ³⁵ Do you not say, 'There are yet four months, then comes the harvest'? Look, I tell you, lift up your eyes, and see that the fields are white for harvest. ³⁶ Already the one who reaps is receiving wages and gathering fruit for eternal life, so that sower and reaper may rejoice together. ³⁷ For here the saying holds true, 'One sows and another reaps.' ³⁸ I sent you to reap that for which you did not labor. Others have labored, and you have entered into their labor."

With some garden crops it is easy to know whether they are ripe and ready to harvest. Tomatoes turn to a soft, glowing, red color, green beans are plump and snap in juicy firmness, while broccoli heads are domed and the florets are green and tight. Then there are the watermelons. Gardeners have various ways of testing melon ripeness. Some look at the underside of the melon for signs of harvest-readiness, others check the tendrils, while others have a mysterious "thump" test.

Jesus refers to the grain harvest. People know when the harvest is ready by communicating with the sower regarding when the crop was planted. It also becomes very evident by the color of the grain that the harvest is near. Jesus tells the disciples that the harvest of souls is ready to be gathered. All they need to do is look around and the need for the harvest is so apparent by the people in need of the Gospel. The sower of the Gospel message can anticipate the harvest because if the Word is preached it will yield a harvest. We are to be sowers of the Gospel message and anticipate a sure harvest.

As Jesus sowed His message, the harvest of eternal life became evident. The disciples were engaged to continue the harvest. We too are commissioned by God to extend the harvest.

Prayer: Dear Lord help us to join in the harvest and share the eternal joy of the fruit of Salvation won by Jesus on the cross of Calvary. In Jesus' name we pray. Amen

The Essence of Gardening and Faith

Text: 1 Corinthians 3:5-9 [5] What then is Apollos? What is Paul? Servants through whom you believed, as the Lord assigned to each. [6] I planted, Apollos watered, but God gave the growth. [7] So neither he who plants nor he who waters is anything, but only God who gives the growth. [8] He who plants and he who waters are one, and each will receive his wages according to his labor. [9] For we are God's fellow workers. You are God's field, God's building.

Gardening can be a humbling experience. We put seeds into the ground, we water, we fertilize, and then we must wait. We wait for the miracle of growth. There is nothing we can do to cause the seed to germinate. Only if the seed contains the miraculous, God-given germ of life, can it send out a sprout and emerge from the soil. Not all seeds germinate. We gardeners can only follow the correct procedures and the essence of life must take over. Some of us are good at sowing the rows straight and true. Others can carefully weed and keep the rows clean. We all have special talents.

Sharing God's Word is much like gardening. We can tell the Gospel message, we can give the Word of Life to others, but only the miracle of faith can save souls eternally. Only God can give the growth. Not all who are touched by the Word spring to faith. Yet we all have special talents to be used in God's garden. Some of us can preach, some of us serve peoples' physical needs, and others have the special gift of prayer.

Prayer: Dear Lord, help us to plant the seeds of the Word of Life abundantly, to assure a large harvest of souls. In Jesus' name we pray. Amen.

33

Imperishable Seed

Text: 1Peter 1: 23-25 ^{23} **since you have been born again, not of perishable seed but of imperishable, through the living and abiding word of God;** ^{24} **for "All flesh is like grass and all its glory like the flower of grass. The grass withers, and the flower falls,** ^{25} **but the word of the Lord remains forever."**

Those of us who garden in northern areas are especially aware of the the seasons. All of the plants, flowers, vegetables, and other flora flourish for a time but then must inevitably perish and wilt as the growing season ends. The grass withers and the flowers fall to the ground.

All flesh, that is to say all earthly life is like the plants in the fall of the year. All life comes to an earthly end. Yet, the word of the Lord remains just as it has since the Garden of Eden. God's promise of a way to eternal life, given to Adam and Eve, continued through the Patriarchs of the Old Testament, was protected through the lineage of David, and was fulfilled in the life, death, and resurrection of Jesus. Now that word continues in the Church and all believers remain forever in faith and salvation. Indeed, the Word of God remains forever.

Prayer: Dear Lord, we thank You for Your eternal Word. We pray that Your Spirit would keep us in that eternal Word and in faith. In Jesus' Name we pray. Amen.

34

Good Soil

Mark 4:20 **²⁰ But those that were sown on the good soil are the ones who hear the word and accept it and bear fruit, thirtyfold and sixtyfold and a hundredfold."**

All of us gardeners want to have good soil in which to garden. We add organic matter; we till in all sorts of plant material and manure to add tilth and nutrients to our gardens. The depth, workability, and richness of our gardens gives us great hope for a bountiful harvest.

Jesus, having grown up around farmers and fishermen knew much about soil. He knew that it made a difference if the soil was rich and deep or thin and rocky. He also knew that His words of life and salvation often fell upon different types of hearers, just as seed was often sown on rich and also on poor soil. Some hearers took the message and acted upon it in a positive way, others absorbed little of His message. Just like the differing results gardeners achieve in poor or rich soil, the results differed among different hearers of the Word.

We, as Christians must enrich our senses and open our hearts to His Word. The results will be like gardening in rich and abundant soil as we bear spiritual fruit.

Prayer: Dear Lord, enrich our hearts with Your Holy Spirit, that we may bear abundant fruit and help grow Your eternal Kingdom. In Jesus name we pray. Amen.

Bearing Fruit and Growing

Text Colossians 1:5-6 [5] the faith and love that spring from the hope stored up for you in heaven and about which you have already heard in the true message of the gospel [6] that has come to you. In the same way, the gospel is bearing fruit and growing throughout the whole world—just as it has been doing among you since the day you heard it and truly understood God's grace.

As we plant our vegetable gardens, fruit trees, and other plants, the hoped-for outcome is for these plants to bear fruit. We put them into the ground with the faith that they will grow and give a return of fresh produce. We tend these plants and do everything we can to help them to grow and bear fruit.

As Paul reached out with the Gospel message to the known world of his time, he also prayed that the "word of truth, the Gospel," would be heard and believed. In these verses written to the Colossian church, Paul is giving thanks for the fruits of faith evident in the congregation there. He has planted and tended the church and now it has borne fruit. Paul tended his plantings as is evident by the many letters he wrote to build up and admonish his churches.

What is most amazing is that Paul's preaching has produced incredible fruit in the whole world. In the years since Jesus ascended into heaven the "words of truth" have gone viral. After the Spirit was out-poured on Pentecost, the Apostles went forth into all the world and boldly preached the Gospel message. The fruits of that preaching were evident in the churches established in Asia and Europe and throughout the Roman Empire. From a small band of plain folks, the number of believers grew miraculously. The fruits of the Gospel message led to forgiveness, faith, and Salvation.

Prayer: Dear Lord bless our efforts to share your Gospel. Send your Spirit to increase the yields of all who plant your word into the hearts of Mankind. In Jesus' name we pray. Amen.

36

Harvesting What We Plant, in Due Season

Text: Galatians 6:7-9 **⁷ Do not be deceived: God cannot be mocked. A man reaps what he sows. ⁸ Whoever sows to please their flesh, from the flesh will reap destruction; whoever sows to please the Spirit, from the Spirit will reap eternal life. ⁹ Let us not become weary in doing good, for at the proper time we will reap a harvest if we do not give up.**

Gardeners all know the importance of planting good seed. We also know how important it is to plant at the correct time. We plant cool weather loving vegetables to mature during the cooler part of the summer. We know that melons and tomatoes like to ripen during the warmer parts of the summer. Each perennial fruit ripens at its proper time; strawberries in early summer, raspberries during the summer and fall months, and apples in the fall season. If we plan our harvest correctly and plant at the right time, we will be rewarded with a good harvest. We cannot expect a good harvest if we plant at the wrong times or if we plant varieties that will not mature properly in our climate and weather patterns.

God tells us that the things that we do in life; the behavior that we pursue determines the outcome of our lives. We must adhere to the Spirit Who breaths faith and forgiveness into our life. In addition to faith we must do good, for it is a connection to the salvation won for us by Christ. Living the Christian life is like planting the correct varieties and if we are patient, as all gardeners learn to become; we will reap the harvest of salvation as promised by our Savior Jesus.

Prayer: Dear Lord, help us to sow to the Spirit, to love a life devoted to good and to faith. Bless us with the eternal harvest that has been won for us through Christ. In Jesus' Name we pray. Amen

37

God's Garden

Reading: Mark 4:26-29 [26] And he said, "The kingdom of God is as if a man should scatter seed on the ground. [27] He sleeps and rises night and day, and the seed sprouts and grows; he knows not how. [28] The earth produces by itself, first the blade, then the ear, then the full grain in the ear. [29] But when the grain is ripe, at once he puts in the sickle, because the harvest has come."

Those of us who grow gardens know that we go to the soil and plant seed into it. We know the seed is hard and without life when we put it into the soil. Yet somehow the interaction of moisture and warmth cause the seed to germinate, to send up green shoots and to grow into a valuable and usable crop. Only patience and the time the seed is in the ground eventually allow us to see the crop rise from the soil. There is nothing we can do to cause the seed to sprout. We must only wait.

God's Kingdom is the same. We can only teach the Word of God and pray that the Holy Spirit will enable that Word to sprout faith in peoples' hearts. That faith grows miraculously. Just as a garden crop is harvested when it is mature, so God's crop of souls will be harvested on Judgment Day.

Prayer: Dear Lord thank you for the faith you have sprouted in our hearts. We pray the harvest will be large as faith sprouts in the hearts of those who hear the Word of Life. In Jesus' name we pray. Amen.

38

Picking Fruit

Text: Galatians 5:22-23 [22] **But the fruit of the Spirit is love, joy, peace, forbearance, kindness, goodness, faithfulness,** [23] **gentleness and self-control. Against such things there is no law.**

There are many things we enjoy in our gardens. The flowers we grow bring color, fragrance, and joy to our world. Herbs in our garden flavor our food and give it character. Fresh vegetables enhance our diet and bring special goodness to our tables. Yet there is probably nothing more enjoyable during our gardening season than the fruits we harvest. Strawberries are a special desert. Raspberries sweeten our summer. Watermelons and cantaloupes are a special summer treat for both young and old. Apples and other tree fruits crown the growing season with their special flavors.

Our text tells about fruits in the Christian life. These are fruits of the Spirit. The list is long and each of these fruits bring a very special element to the Christian life. Study these fruits, get to know them, and savor their wonderful contributions in our daily lives. Then we must consider the greatest fruit given to us. It is the fruit of Christ's work on earth. Through the work of Redemption accomplished by Jesus' life, death, and resurrection, we are given Salvation and the fruit of being with Christ eternally.

Prayer: Dear Lord, we thank you for the fruits of the Spirit. Help us to give and partake of these fruits. Thank You especially for the eternal fruit of salvation. In Jesus' name we pray. Amen.

39

The Gardener's Reward

Text: 1Corinthians 3:6-9 **⁶ I planted, Apollos watered, but God gave the growth. ⁷ So neither he who plants nor he who waters is anything, but only God who gives the growth. ⁸ He who plants and he who waters are one, and each will receive his wages according to his labor. ⁹ For we are God's fellow workers. You are God's field, God's building.**

Gardeners spend many hours tilling, marking rows, and planting seeds in their soil. Money is spent to buy seeds, plants, and fertilizer. The garden is planned during the winter and all of the gardener's hope and expectations hinge upon germination and growth. Water is applied to get things off to a good start and the gardener then must do what is most difficult: he must wait for growth. What if the growth doesn't occur? What if nothing germinates and nothing grows? The gardener must then wonder what good he has done.

Without the mysterious miracle of growth all the gardener's work is in vain. The gardener would feel insignificant, almost useless, because nothing came up, nothing grew. There is a miracle that must take place. It is a miracle of sun, warmth, soil-life, and moisture. Only if these miracles take place can the gardener feel that all of his efforts have been worthwhile.

As God's servants we can proclaim God's Word, we can pray for those who we expose to the Word, we can teach the doctrine of the church, but only God can work faith in people's hearts. Only the Holy Spirit can complete our efforts and open the hearts of believers to the gift of forgivingness and Salvation. The greatest joy to the gardener is the harvest and as Christians we rejoice in the harvest of souls made possible by the Word we are given and the Holy Spirit who works through the Word.

Prayer: Dear Lord we thank You for the bountiful harvest given as a result of our planting of the Word. In Jesus' Name we pray. Amen

40

A Full Freezer

Text: Luke 12:16-21 [16] And he told them a parable, saying, "The land of a rich man produced plentifully, [17] and he thought to himself, 'What shall I do, for I have nowhere to store my crops?' [18] And he said, 'I will do this: I will tear down my barns and build larger ones, and there I will store all my grain and my goods. [19] And I will say to my soul, "Soul, you have ample goods laid up for many years; relax, eat, drink, be merry."' [20] But God said to him, 'Fool! This night your soul is required of you, and the things you have prepared, whose will they be?' [21] So is the one who lays up treasure for himself and is not rich toward God."

Both my wife and I grew up in gardening families. When we got married we wanted to grow our own food. The first summer we planted a large garden and enjoyed fresh peas, green beans, broccoli, potatoes, tomatoes, and all the other wonderful delights of the summer garden. Such an abundance of food became ours, that we decided to buy a deep freezer and bought ever-increasing numbers of canning jars. The harvest kept coming and we kept preserving food for the winter months.

As newlyweds we had little idea of how much food we could eat in one winter. We stored grocery bags full of frozen green beans, jars of canned tomatoes and tomato sauce lined our shelves. Sauerkraut and pickles of all shapes and sizes filled our little storage room. We became obsessed with our food stores. It consumed us more than we could consume vegetables. The realization became evident, when by mid-winter we had hardly made a dent in our food stores.

What were we thinking? Having spent most available hours preserving food during that summer, we missed the whole point of enjoying summer to its fullest. As we donated food to our school's hot lunch program that winter, we realized the futility of becoming obsessed with storing up earthly goods. Earthly preparations are appropriate but not at the expense of spiritual grounding.

One day, and we don't know when it will come, our souls will be required of us. All the jars of vegetables on the shelf will have little effect upon the condition of our souls. As much as we love our gardens and our produce, we need to include God in our daily life.

Prayer: Dear Lord, send us Your Spirit to ever-remind us that You must be the center of our life. Help us be ever-mindful that the greatest fruits of all were produced on the Cross of Calvary as Jesus provided for our eternal welfare. In Jesus' Name we pray. Amen

41

Watering Our Garden

Text: Isaiah 35: 1-4 The wilderness and the dry land shall be glad; the desert shall rejoice and blossom like the crocus; ² it shall blossom abundantly and rejoice with joy and singing. The glory of Lebanon shall be given to it, the majesty of Carmel and Sharon. They shall see the glory of the LORD, the majesty of our God. ³ Strengthen the weak hands, and make firm the feeble knees. ⁴ Say to those who have an anxious heart, "Be strong; fear not! Behold, your God will come with vengeance, with the recompense of God. He will come and save you."

I remember gardening in a rather arid area. Only by constant watering could I accomplish a lush garden. The soil was good and as water was introduced it became green and productive.

The verses in Isaiah point to a time of greening, with abundant plants springing up. From Mt. Carmel on the north to the fertile Plain of Sharon along the Mediterranean Coast abundant rain falls, which usher in the great bounty of crops produced in the area. The crocus is a flower that springs to life as the rains water these bountiful plains.

The people of Israel knew of the abundance of this area and Isaiah says this is the abundance that will spring forth in the time of the coming Messiah. The words ring true as we celebrate the Christmas miracle during this winter season; the coming of the Messiah to earth. God sent Jesus to save us just as was foretold by the prophet Isaiah.

Prayer: Dear Lord we thank you for bringing the lush blessings of new life and eternal goodness to us through the Bethlehem Baby of Christmas. In Jesus' name we pray. Amen.

42

The Blessing of Good Land

Text: Ezekiel 36:27-30 **27** And I will put my Spirit within you, and cause you to walk in my statutes and be careful to obey my rules. **28** You shall dwell in the land that I gave to your fathers, and you shall be my people, and I will be your God. **29** And I will deliver you from all your uncleannesses. And I will summon the grain and make it abundant and lay no famine upon you. **30** I will make the fruit of the tree and the increase of the field abundant, that you may never again suffer the disgrace of famine among the nations.

There is no greater gift from God than the land and the abundance that it can produce. Gardeners know what a great blessing there is in a plot of fertile ground. A fifty-foot square plot of good, rich soil can provide food for a family, if well-tended.

In the Old Testament God promised Abraham land. It was land that would be home to Abraham and his descendants. Being blessed with this land would also mean that Abraham and his descendants would also be a blessing to all mankind. For out of this land and people would come the Savior.

Israel, by disobedience to God, lost the land; lost the very essence of their identity. Yet here the prophet Ezekiel prophesies that God's Spirit will again return to the people of Israel. They would again dwell in the land of their fathers. The land would again be fruitful and produce abundant crops. Most important-ly, from these descendants of Abraham, through the family of David, the Savior Jesus would come to the world. Through the blessing of repentance and forgiveness the path to Salvation for all, would be through the land of Israel. The Savior born in Beth-lehem would be for all mankind.

Prayer: Dear Lord, thank You for being a patient God, who calls His people back, and through forgiveness carries out the great promise of a Messiah to save us eternally. We pray in Jesus' name. Amen.

43

Fresh Melons in December

Text: Psalms 145:15-16 **¹⁵ The eyes of all look to you, and you give them their food in due season. ¹⁶ You open your hand; you satisfy the desire of every living thing.**

Here is a devotion title to excite gardeners. In most areas of the United States, freshly-picked melons in December are mostly out of the question. December is just not the season for picking melons in North America. Gardeners realize there is a season for most things. We look for apples in the late summer and fall. We count on our asparagus to start popping up in the first warm spring weather for one of our earliest vegetable delights.

As the Psalmist writes, we look to God for each season and depend upon the seasons to produce the fruits that are appropriate. God opens His hand and gives us what we need. Gardeners, perhaps more than anyone, see the rhythm and bounty of the seasons.

Just as God takes care of our physical needs with the seasons, so too we see that He has also taken care of our spiritual needs. He has given us His life-giving Word in the Bible. Most importantly He sent His Son to be the perfect sacrifice for all of our sins, ensuring us of life and eternal salvation.

Prayer: Dear Lord, we give thanks for the abundant seasons. Send us Your Holy Spirit to strengthen our faith and assure us of our salvation in Christ. In Jesus' name we pray. Amen.

44

Remain and Watch

Text: John 18:1-2 ¹ When he had finished praying, Jesus left with his disciples and crossed the Kidron Valley. On the other side there was a garden, and he and his disciples went into it. ² Now Judas, who betrayed him, knew the place, because Jesus had often met there with his disciples.

Mark 14:32-34 ³² They went to a place called Gethsemane, and Jesus said to his disciples, "Sit here while I pray." ³³ He took Peter, James and John along with him, and he began to be deeply distressed and troubled. ³⁴ "My soul is overwhelmed with sorrow to the point of death," he said to them. "Stay here and keep watch."

Where do we gardeners go when we need solitude, time to contemplate, perhaps even prayer time? Of course, our gardens are a source of comfort for us. They give us the physical and emotional outlet that we need.

Jesus too found the garden of Gethsemane a place of reflection. It is where He went to pray when the most trying time lay ahead. The disciples knew the place as well. They met there with Jesus to be instructed and prepared for the work ahead of them. They could not know for certain what was ahead. Yet the powerful words of Jesus spoken in the quietude of the garden would reverberate in their minds as the Spirit led them to teach and preach and write down the words of life taught them by their Savior.

In the time of great sorrow just before His capture and crucifixion, Jesus took the disciples one last time to the garden and instructed them to remain and watch. As Jesus prayed for strength to endure the cross, perhaps the disciples found a source of strengthening as well.

We too, need to remain and watch. We need to learn the earnestness of Jesus' prayer and perhaps go to our own places of solace to pray and be strengthened. Our gardens are not only places of beauty but also places of prayer and reflection.

Prayer: Dear Lord, give us the comfort and strength we need as we pray in our special quiet places. In Jesus Name we pray. Amen.

45

Don't Be Anxious

Text Philippians 4:6-7 **⁶ do not be anxious about anything, but in everything by prayer and supplication with thanksgiving let your requests be made known to God. ⁷ And the peace of God, which surpasses all understanding, will guard your hearts and your minds in Christ Jesus.**

I have been a gardener for most of my life and a vegetable farmer for a great many years. If there is any group of people who can find reasons to be anxious it is farmers and gardeners. The questions can fill our waking hours and can keep us awake at night. Will we get enough rain? Will we get too much rain? Which insect pests will come to visit? Which disease problems will attack my crops? Will it be warm enough to mature my warmth–loving crops? Will it be too hot for crops that like more moderate weather? Will late frost in spring damage early-planted crops? Will early frost in the fall cut the yield of some crops? Will that old piece of farm machinery hold up for another season?

By now most gardeners get the message, because there are so many questions and worries that can dance in the minds of growers. In Philippians Chapter Four, we are admonished to not be anxious about anything but to pray with thanksgiving in our hearts. We can focus upon the good crops in the past or deliverance from pests that have been successfully avoided or remedied. We must not allow questions and doubts to cloud our attitude. After all, the greatest thing in the world to be thankful for is the salvation won for us by Christ and given to us freely on the wings of faith. Faith in all matters, can give us the peace of God which indeed surpasses all understanding. The eternal hope will guard our hearts and minds in Christ Jesus.

Prayer: Dear Lord be with us in all our daily struggles and send us your Spirit to pick us up and give us Your peace. In Jesus' name we pray. Amen

46

Finding Good Seed

Text: 1Peter 1:23-25 ²³ since you have been born again, not of perishable seed but of imperishable, through the living and abiding word of God; ²⁴ for "All flesh is like grass and all its glory like the flower of grass. The grass withers, and the flower falls, ²⁵ but the word of the Lord remains forever." And this word is the good news that was preached to you.

There are truths to be learned in the garden. As we search seed sources for our next year's garden we are always conscious of finding good reliable seed companies. Those who grow gardens, know what it is like to work up the soil, plant seed and then wait and wait, finally to realize that the seed they have planted is just not going to come up. It is old, or has lost its vigor. The work was in vain. Gardeners also know that even the most beautiful garden eventually withers, the flowers fade, and they are gone.

What a joy for Christians to know that the Word of God is imperishable. The Word that is preached to us by our pastors is the imperishable seed; the living and enduring Word of God. It is the Word of Life; an eternal life never to wither or fade.

Prayer: Dear Lord, we thank You for the eternal Word that is ours. We pray that we continually are able to hear and share this eternal gift of the Word. In Jesus' name we pray. Amen

47

Succession Planting

Text: Galatians 6:9 ⁹ And let us not grow weary of doing good, for in due season we will reap, if we do not give up.

I remember one gardening season I planted green beans. As soon as they came up a bunch of pesky gophers ate all the young sprouts. I re-worked the soil and planted beans again, only to have hot, dry, weather devastate the crop. Once more I planted. After the third planting a timely rain brought a nice stand of young plants, which grew rapidly in the long summer days. By early fall, I had a huge crop of beautiful beans to harvest.

As Christians we have probably all experienced disappointment when we have witnessed to others. We may have witnessed by acts of kindness or generosity, or in other ways expressed our faith to them. Yet often we see little interest in our faith among others to whom we witness.

Paul tells us to not grow weary of doing good. Just as God blesses our perseverance in the garden, he will also bless us with a response to our Christian witness.

Payer: Dear Lord, help us to not grow weary of doing good and help us persevere in Your will. In Jesus' name we pray. Amen.

Glorified Seed

Text: John 12: 23-25 [23] And Jesus answered them, "The hour has come for the Son of Man to be glorified. [24] Truly, truly, I say to you, unless a grain of wheat falls into the earth and dies, it remains alone; but if it dies, it bears much fruit.[25] Whoever loves his life loses it, and whoever hates his life in this world will keep it for eternal life.

Winter is a time of dormancy, when perennial plants and many seeds lie in the ground waiting for a new season. Jesus' words often teach a simple truth connected to the land. He often speaks about seed and there is much to be learned from seed. Some of us gardeners harvest seed and save it to be used in our next garden. If we save bean seeds from some wonderful heirloom variety, we can reap a harvest from the seed in a following season. Of course, seed that we save to plant cannot be eaten. It is not used but saved to be put into the ground where it will actually die in the process of bringing forth new life and a more beautiful and abundant result than if we had just used it as food.

Jesus teaches us the meaning of life and salvation as He is about to be put to death. He says that He is about to be glorified. Only by his death can He and all of us be glorified. Just as seed that goes into the ground is resurrected, so Christ and all believers are resurrected to a more abundant and eternal life.

Prayer: Dear Lord, thank You for the lesson taught through the miracle of seed. Thank You especially for glorifying Jesus through His death and resurrection, leading the way for all believers to salvation. In Jesus' name we pray. Amen

49

The Mustard Seed

Text: Mark 13:31-33 **³¹** **He put another parable before them, saying, "The kingdom of heaven is like a grain of mustard seed that a man took and sowed in his field.** **³²** **It is the smallest of all seeds, but when it has grown it is larger than all the garden plants and becomes a tree, so that the birds of the air come and make nests in its branches."**

The very essence of gardening is growth. We don't plant seeds and expect to keep watch upon a piece of land that stays bare and empty for the whole summer. We gardeners anticipate a new sprout emerging from the soil. We expect that sprout to appear quickly. We feed that sprout with fertilizer, remove competitive weeds, and water when needed. Gardening is all about seeing the plants grow, get larger, flower, and in the case of vegetables, produce fruit. A tomato plant for instance can reach several feet tall, and spread across ten to fifteen square feet of land. Although the seed is small it can produce quite a large plant in just one summer.

Jesus taught about the mustard seed, which is a small seed, yet germinates and grows quickly. It becomes a large plant and, in some instances, it is large enough that birds can nest in its branches. Our Lord draws a lesson from the fast-growing plant.

It is like the Kingdom of Heaven. Jesus came to earth in a small and obscure way. His followers were not royalty or great political figures of His time. The small and the obscure would grow rapidly. Now we see how the Christian message has spread across the whole globe. Just as the miracle of the tiny mustard seed is evident, so the miracle of faith and salvation through Christ's redeeming work has overspread the world. Jesus foretold this miracle with a simple parable and we can see the fulfillment of His prophecy as the world church of Christians grows.

Prayer: Dear Lord, we thank you for the "mustard seed" of Jesus' work on earth and pray that we as Christians can continue to cultivate His Word of Life. In Jesus' name we pray. Amen

50

The Garden of our Salvation

Text: John 19:40-42 **⁴⁰ So they took the body of Jesus and bound it in linen cloths with the spices, as is the burial custom of the Jews. ⁴¹ Now in the place where he was crucified there was a garden, and in the garden a new tomb in which no one had yet been laid. ⁴² So because of the Jewish day of Preparation, since the tomb was close at hand, they laid Jesus there.**

It was the end of a horrendous day for the followers of Jesus. After having to watch their Lord and Savior tortured and crucified, they needed a place to put the body and prepare it for burial. After all the trauma of that day which we call "Good Friday," they are directed to a garden and a tomb. Here the body of their crucified Lord is laid. In the garden, the peace of their Lord is assured. The garden is the resting place of our Lord, as the work of Salvation is carried out.

The best is yet to come, for in that garden the miraculous resurrection of our Savior has its earthly completion. Here He shows himself to Mary Magdalene. In this peaceful setting, where she first mistook her Lord for a gardener, the miracle of the Resurrection is displayed. Indeed, God works some of His greatest miracles in gardens.

Each time we gardeners go to our gardens we need to remember that peaceful garden of the Resurrection.

Prayer: Dear Lord we thank You for gardens, especially the wonderful garden of the Resurrection. Fill us with Your peace and love as we garden. In Jesus' name we pray. Amen.

www.ingramcontent.com/pod-product-compliance
Lightning Source LLC
LaVergne TN
LVHW021537080426
835509LV00019B/2688